Furrows of Fancy

My plough is a pen,
And my seed is a thought;
I plough and sow;
Then, behold, in my plot,
"Furrows of Fancy"

BY

James Gordon O'Neill

To Dee

Jim O'Neill
Grandpa

6-7-03

ISBN: 0-7596-8816-8

This book is printed on acid free paper.

1stBooks - rev. 2/25/02

Preface

While I have lived seventy of my ninety-two years in the city, I am still a farm boy at heart, thus; many of my poems have rural settings and deal with natural phenomena.

I feel that my poetry displays my generally optimistic yet realistic view of life and, if the reader derives pleasure from reading it, I shall be deeply gratified.

October 2001

Index

1- Why Art Thou Cast Down

Why art thou cast down, 0 my soul?

Is it, perchance, the high cost of petrol?

Or is it the daily traffic grid

That we so fervently wish to rid?

Or is it the stock market's plummet

From the high mark of its summit?

Or is it the stormy winter weather

When we're getting near the end of our tether?

Or is it only a pain in the stomach's pit

That makes us stop and think a bit?

Cheer up, my soul, and vanish fear

Better times may come now any year.

04/03/01

2- The Happy Farmer

I was raised a farmer's son
And I did what a farmer does;
I fed the cows and cleaned the stalls
And still found the time for fun.

I fed the cackling hens
And gathered up their eggs;
I whistled a merry tune
As I cleaned up their pens.

I ignored their steady squeal
And muted my sense of smell
As I slopped the ravenous pigs
With their stable daily meal.

I curried my faithful mares
And brushed their glossy coats;
I was generous with their oats
For they were loyal confreres.

So we learn from the farmer's son
Who was a most contented fellow
Our joy from life is all that matters
When all is said and done.

31/12/00

3- Barefoot Memories

When I was once a barefoot boy
I had no cares and boundless joy;
The feel of dust between my toes
Is a memory that forever grows.

I knew where wild strawberries grew
I knew when the black caps were due
And my barefeet would direct me
To the very places I wished to be.

Thoughts of colonies of honey bees
Ensconced in the tall hollow trees
And shaggy bark of the hickory tree
Bring pleasant boyhood memories to me.

When each happy day was ending
And darkness fast descending
No day was quite complete
Till mother called. "Come boys, wash your feet."

09/05/00

4- Yeah Grandpa

Though most of *my* years are spent,
I'm a most irrepressible gent;
And to tell you the truth
I think very much like a youth.

My grandchildren with their appeal
Have greatly influenced how 1 feel;
And how I love their young friends
With all their modern trends!

Were I to live over again
I'd maintain youth's optimistic yen;
For I love the zest of young folk
And the thoughts that they provoke.

29/08/00

5- Memories

As seasons come
And seasons go:
All the while
My memories grow.

I catch a flash
Of my boyhood home:
The fields and woods
I used to roam.

I hear the sound
Of frogs in Spring,
And smell the scent
Fruit blossoms bring.

The wooden pump,
So hard to prime,
Gave crystal water
Every time.

The old rain barrel
Under the eave,
Branded on my mind,
Will never leave.

The old gray mares
I used to drive
Keep my rural
Past alive.

And thus it is
That year by year
My fondest Mem'ries
become more clear.

02~12IOO

6- Transition

As September slowly puts summer to rest,
She beckons Autumn to be her guest.
The season, as by some wondrous design
Slowly and surely falls into steady decline.

The fields that waved with golden grain
Lie bare and thirsting for the Autumn rain;
And trees whose foliage lately lush and green,
Are changing dress to match the Autumn scene.

The birds that sang in the earlier times
Form flocks to fly to southern climes;
Butterflies that fluttered under sunny skies
Have spun cocoons and bide their time in true disguise.

But, if we have the patience to wait,
The birds will sing at the proper date,
And Spring will spread such a garment of green
That forest and field will form a magnificent scene.

04/08/00

7- My Beloved

"There's a Place in my heart."
That cannot be filled;
There's a voice in my soul
That cannot be stilled:
For love is a thing that lives on
Though the loved one be gone

I'm still longing for the old days,
And dreaming of the old ways,
When my beloved would smile at me:
And oh! How happy we would be!

Though there's a spot in my heart
That cannot be filled:
With fond memories of those times
My whole being is thrilled

15/07/00

8- The Ultimate Dichotomy

An old person looks back

And a young person looks forward;

Which gets the greater pleasure

Is most difficult to measure.

The old person's views are static;

The young person's quite erratic.

The old person speaks with definite conviction;

The young person's thoughts are nebulous as fiction.

In between these two stages

Are the persons of all other ages;

Some are wise and some are foolish;

Some are stubborn and even mulish

Yet, out of this diversity of population

We have built a cohesive nation.

31/05/00

9- Bless Our Land

O Canada, we sing of thee
Our land so blest and free;
Your sons and daughters cheer
The land they all hold dear.

From northern tundra's snow
Where wild winds rage and blow
To Point Pelee's southern tip
Words of praise are on each lip.

From B.C's tall red pines
To Nova Scotia's ancient mines
Your people feel a sense of pride
|That lesser nations are denied.

God bless our land from sea to sea
And may this be our fervent plea
That all your citizens shall strive
To keep your proud name alive.

O Canada 'tis of thee we sing;
Loud may our praises ring!
And let our voices all unite
To keep our land a shining light.

08/04/00

10- Winding Down

Dear Lord, I'm winding down

And I'm just coasting home.

At ninety-one

My race is nearly done

And I am just coasting home.

I don't deserve a crown

For good deeds that I have done;

But through my omissions

I have let good persons down

And for this, I'm truly sorry;

And for this, I may have missed the Land of Glory!

Any way, dear Lord, I'm winding down

And I'm slowly coasting home.

29/01/00

11- A Global Attitude

You ask me what is on my mind
And I answer: all mankind.
For I'm in a broad expansive mood
And a friendly global attitude.

I'm told the "Group of Eight" has met
And our deteriorating environment may yet
Survive the nations' careless ways
And earn our children's grateful praise.

I've read that many countries have stated
What dreadful havoc land mines have created;
An anti-landmine treaty that was signed,
When ratified, will benefit all mankind.

So when you ask me what is on my mind
'Tis mostly environmental things I find;
And leaders of the world are finally aware:
It is about these matters people care.

04/00

12- The Bobolink

The melodious song of the bobolink
Turns back my thoughts to boyhood days
When meadows smelled of clover blossoms
And life was simple in all its ways.

And oh! That I might as joyous be
As I was, when first, the bobolink excited me;
In flight, it's sweet trebled notes
Filled my young soul with glee.

The memory of these boyhood years
Is the link that stabilizes me;
And the bobolink, God bless it,
Keeps my aging vision free.

07/07/98

13- Time and Space

I am time: I roll irresistibly on:
For me a century is but a yawn;
Millenniums go by without respite;
Whole eras pass like a flash of light.

Puny man cries out "Hey! Wait!
Why race on at this dizzying rate?
Let 'Three score and Ten years' be still
So I may contemplate God's will."

I am space: I have no known bounds:
I stretch beyond the periphery of sounds.
The galaxies of the Milky Way can't fill me
For I can expand to infinity.

Again man cries out in deep despair,
"Where does humanity fit in? Where? Oh where!"
The answer to the question is very terse:
"Man can never solve the mystery of the universe."

16/03/98

14- What A Wonderful World

Nature is so well designed
No defect in it can one find;
From Milky Way to finest sand
All seem to be superbly planned.

Regularly the seasons come and go;
In summer rain; in winter snow;
Day follows night; night follows day;
Thus, on and on, in an orderly way.

The puffy clouds in the August sky
Display perfection to the human eye;
One marvels at God's infinite scheme
And acknowledges His works to be supreme.

From little ants that build their mound,
To earthworms that live underground,
The universe is full of tiny wonders;
Divine wisdom could tolerate no blunders.

The feathered bird and the furry beast,
From the greatest to the very least,
Perform their various functions well
And procreate from a single cell.

James Gordon O'Neill

As the sun sets the clock on another day,
The moon tracks the sky on its circular way
The stars peer out from the firmament's dome
And light the ceiling of their Creator's home.

1996

15- The Maple Leaf

May the maple leaf forever
Adorn our nation's flag
And may we never, never
Let our patriotism lag.

May our citizens' endeavour
Make our land so endeared
That the maple leaf forever
Shall be loved and never feared.

May the maple leaf so stir our pride
At every international event
That all the nations far and wide
Will sense how much our emblem meant.

20/03/98

16- Precious Moments

Precious moments! Oh, what precious moments!

Those moments just before I have to rise!

As I cuddle down, seconds are at a premium,

And I realize how flippantly times flies.

Precious moments! I savour those moments:

The ones just before I have to rise.

Oh that time would just stand still

To prolong the pleasure the clock denies.

Precious moments! I treasure those moments:

Those moments full of serenity and peace;

But since they can not last forever

When duty calls, the precious moments cease.

Duty calls! Precious moments not withstanding,

I must divest my warm and cozy bed;

But since 'tis only till next morning

I slowly pull the covers round my head.

Precious moments! Such precious moments

Form a happy prelude to another day.

At once so beautiful and short-lived!

Would that they could with me much longer stay!

28/12/99

17- The Vacant Chair

The vacant chair sits where she sat
Where my beloved and I would often chat;
But now she's gone and I labour on,
I have but memories to think upon.
Fond memories spread o'er sixty years
Remind me of times of joy and tears.
Pleasure and sorrow we faced as a team
And our love flowed on in a steady stream.
Times like the past can ne'er return
No matter how hard my heart may yearn.
But how I cherish the thoughts I share
When e'er I gaze upon that dear old chair.

1996

18- The Primary

Five rows,
Eight seats each;
Forty little souls
To teach.

Wee girls,
Mother's pearls;
Sweetly brushing back
Their curls.

Wee boys,
Their father's joys;
Discipline disrupts
Their poise.

Each one,
Parents pet;
Nothing evil in
It yet.

Teacher,
You are blest;
Drawing out of each
His best.

Your job,

Making men;

Worthy one, too, isn't

It then.

16/08/37

19- Reflections of an Old Man

When I was young I held my tongue
And did not contradict my elders;
But now that I'm old, I've grown bold
And question opinions of old and young.

When I was young, I was quite naïve
And, thus it was, I was quick to believe;
But now I'm old, I require sure proof;
And when not forthcoming, I stand aloof.

When I was young, I was so unsophisticated
I was a nerd to all the girls I dated;
But now I'm old, I'm a model of culture
And ladies swarm round me like a hungry vulture.

When I was young, I was ambitious
And knew no reason to be suspicious;
But now I'm old and chronically lazy
I even suspect that some of my age are crazy.

19/09/99

20- A Morning in May

It's great to be alive on a morning like this,
Just to feel the sun's warm gentle kiss,
To breathe the perfume of the blossoming trees
And sense the caress of the gentle breeze.

All creatures endured the winter storm
Knowing well the buds of spring would form
And beauty pervade the earth once more
As it has in myriads of springs before.

Let the birds sing and the blossoms swell
For, like them we know that all is well;
The world is unfolding as it should
In field and garden and early wood.

Let our hearts and souls rejoice;
Burst forth with a happy voice;
Our whole spirit should echo the bliss
Of being alive on a morning like this.

1997

21- Freedom and Fancy

Freedom and Fancy, together,
Are ever a frolicsome pair,
For they know no bound nor tether;
Neither know they rest nor care.

They sail the seas together
In a seashell for a boat
And no matter what the weather
That seashells keeps afloat.

They pluck a pretty feather
From a proud old peacock's tail
And they use that pretty feather
To serve as mast and sail.

With a sailor fore and aft,
And their feather in the breeze,
That fearless little craft
Sails o'er the seven seas.

They sail to hills of heather
Near the shores of fairyland
And they trip along together
Down the valleys hand in hand.

They mount a darning-needle
And they rasp upon its wings
Till they fairly make them tweedle
Like a golden harp with strings.

They soar quite up to heaven
To engage the Angels, bright,
That they come and sweetly leaven
All wee children's dreams that night.

01/08/39

22- My Wife

There's no girl like the one who darns my socks;

Oh yes I like the girl who darns my socks.

Before that I got double, socks gave uncommon trouble,

But now that I've a wife, there's new joy come to my life;

I recall the life I led, in the days before I wed,

And then for joy I sing of the day I bought the ring,

For there's no girl like the girl that darns my socks.

There's no girl like the one who wedded me;

Oh yes, I like the girl that wedded me.

For the tea-pot on the stove is in love with her by jove,

And the pots and pans and all are at her beck and call;

Each one thinks that she is right, so with her unite

To prepare the tasty meal that to me does so appeal;

And there's no girl like the girl that wedded me.

There's no girl like the girl that cares for me;

Oh yes I like the girl who cares for me.

Whene'er we take a trip, I've no more to pack my grip;

Since we've become a pair, I've no dandruff in my hair;

We have money in the banks; 'tis to her I give the thanks;

Oh gee, but isn't it great in the happy married state,

When there's no girl like the one that cares for me.

11/12/36

23- Unnoticed

In every time and clime,
In every age and nation,
Spring up good men sublime,
The choice of God's creation.

And some attain to fame,
And some to endless glory,
Whose lives so free of blame
Are writ in verse and story.

But tens of thousands more,
Sweet roses of desert air,
Mute Miltons at our door,
Leave no print anywhere.

12/09/36

24- The Farm Boy

The farm boy to the barn is gone
With woolen mitts and mackinaw on;
He trots along the snow-packed path,
And like a mighty giant of Gath,

Defies the biting wind and frost;
Without a single moment lost
He soon unbars the great barn doors
And quick as flash begins his chores.

The stallion gives his stall a kick,
His customary morning trick;
The young colts give a gentle neigh
And do their appetites betray;

The old bull clanks his heavy chain,
with mighty strain he's up again,
To bellow forth a lusty grace
Before his meal, a little space.

A brief span and the feeding's done
—Once more his flock's affection's won—
Out to the water trough he goes
To chop the ice with heavy blows;

The ice chips fly both high and wide
Till water splashes on every side;
The cold steel hoop his pant leg claims,
His mitts freeze stiff as harness hames.

The farm boy to the house returns
To where a wood fire brightly burns.
With lowered head and hunched-up back
He hastes along the snowy track;

He hears the phone wires zinging clear
And half-frozen sparrows chirping near;
At last, he nears the farmhouse door,
Quite glad he's done his morning chore.

1937

25- Butterflies

A swarm of fluttering butterflies
Danced gaily past my boyish eyes.
Such youthful joy beamed o'er my face
My impulse was to give them chase
For I had found a lovely prize
Of white and yellow cabbage flies.

They hovered o'er a little pond,
Alighted here or flew beyond;
They circled o'er its grassy edge
And settled at the water's edge.
Oh how I lacked a magic wand
To hold them prisoners on the pond.

Like yachts afloat on a quiet bay
The sparred and rigged flotilla lay;
I eyed that fleet with wonderment
And caught the charm their shyness lent
For I must at my distance stay
To gaze upon that grand display.

1937

26- Gratitude for a Roof

The wailing winds tonight
Make music most forlorn;
I know and feel
That Autumn's seal
Is set upon the morn.

I hear the rushing rains
Descend outside my roof;
I cosy lie,
Both warm and dry,
In chamber water-proof.

I thank Thee heartily,
O God. most merciful,
I am content;
No element,
Can at my sinews pull.

James Gordon O'Neill

27- The Sun

O thou great sustainer of life on this earth,

Thou mighty dispenser of gladness and mirth,

Shine round about us in a radiance to-day;

Dispel all our cares and drive them away.

In winter thou meltest the snow from the steep

And callest the flowers of springtime from sleep;

Wheat fields in summer rejoice in thy smile;

Apples in autumn are ripened the while.

O finest reflection of God that we find,

His greatest physician for suffering mankind,

Pour out upon us with bountiful measure;

Revive all our souls to share in thy pleasure.

1937

28- Fireflies

In the deep, dead silence

Of the forest drenched in dew

While strange shapes lurk

Midst the forest's hazy hue

The fireflies' fitful flashes

Spark from out the ghostly gloom

To signal sleeping fairies

And spirits within the tomb.

1937

29- Ontario's Emblem

Let us sing of Ontario's emblem
And consider its intrinsic right
To be placed above all other plants
With flowers more gaudy and bright.

Frequenting old woodlots and valleys
There, modest, unassuming, she grows
And knowing quite well her right place
She ne'er shall create any foes.

Her flower of white is as pure
As Nature can perfect from earth;
She reveals to Ontario's youth
Those merits of loftiest worth.

Her triple structure oft reminds
Of Father, Son, and Holy Ghost
And gently bids that we should place
Our Christian faith always foremost.

30- Rocks

Like tumors in the bowels of the earth
Buried there from the time of their birth,
Abiding, unmolested through epochs,
Slumber on the great ageless rocks.

And 'twere not for the nature of man
To appropriate all he can,
They might sleep as serenely forever,
Till God, in his time, shouldst sever.

31- Dreams

I like to go to bed and dream
I dwell where courts and castles seem
A common and most natural thing
Wherein I reign as sovereign King.
There, too, within my kingly hall,
I lavish many a stately ball
Where knights and ladies lightly tread
To lays and dances nobly led.
Perhaps, while yet the evening's young,
Some merry minstrel's lays are sung,
Or jesters joke and play the fool
Diverting mighty ones who rule;
And, yonder fencers thrust and tilt
Till skill or trick rich blood has spilt.
Horns of richest wine pass round
And cheers within the hall resound.
Thus, on I dream—most marvellous thing—
That, night by night, I am a king.

1937

32- The Lairds Creed

I'll take God's word for what it's worth
So long as I live upon this earth
And believe that Christ has power to save;
There is a life beyond the grave.

For if there's naught in what He's said
I'll never know it when I'm dead'
But, be it true, as I expect,
I'll be among His own elect.

For those who believe the other way
Will get a jolt on Judgement Day
And being not for such prepared
Will envy the BELIEVING LAIRD.

1937

33- Is This Decadence

There is a man in England yet
Can fill the world with awe,
Can rouse his people's courage,
For they love his bull-dog jaw.

Some folk call him Winnie;
He calls himself Bullfinch.
We know the Nazis call him,
"The man we'd like to lynch".

34- Graves of the Great

Show us the graves of great men
And extol illustrious deeds;
For, generations after him,
The truly great man leads.

And show us, too, the humble grave
And keep alive his worth,
Whose honour, toil, and sacrifice,
Helped give his country birth.

1938

35- In Spring Again

The grass is growing green again;

My mind is more serene again;

The birds are back to build again;

My soul is strangely filled again;

The rose receives the bee again;

While life wells up in me again;

All things in nature live again;

New zest to life they give again;

The spring is such a mystery;

Sweet mystery, sweet mystery;

For life anew pervades me, too,

In Spring again, in Spring again.

36- Men of the Soil

Blest is that man whose daily toil
Is spent upon the fruitful soil;
Majestic is his wrinkled brow
Though rough the hand that guides the plough.

The share and coulter cut and slice
The root and sod by his device;
The shiny mold-board, smoothly bent,
Doth turn the clay with mute assent.

Most blest is he of all his race,
Co-equal with the king and mace;
Co-partner he is with his God,
That man, who turns the crumbling sod.

37- The Chickadee

Thou tiny bit of bird!
Blithest creature e'er I've heard;
Upside down upon a twig,
Of fear, thou carest not a fig.

What a tiny mite of flesh!
Ever blithesome; ever fresh;
How can you so friendly be
While my axe chops down your tree?

Your constant chirping is a perk
That brightens up my weary work;
And I shall ever grateful be
To you, my friendly chickadee.

1995

38- War and Peace

When submarines have ceased to ply
Beneath the blue sea's surface screen
And commerce crosses o'er the waves
And convoys are no longer seen;

When planes no longer from the sky
Blast homes and cities into bits
And populations in their fear
Forsake their subterranean pits;

When monstrous bugs of iron and steel
No longer creep on pillar wheels
And pleasure cars supplant the jeep
On all the motion picture reels;

When lustful lunatics of war
No longer shape their fiery darts;
When minds contrive to kill no more
And coal shall forge for peaceful arts;

When money goes to nurture life
And not to halt or maim or kill,
And all the nations, bound as one,
Shall speak the universal will;

Then, then, ye heroes of a peaceful cause

May clap your hands in grand applause.

39- When I Come to Build my Cottage

When I come to build my cottage
At the sunset of my life,
I shall shun the shallow mob
And this world's woeful strife.

When I come to build my cottage
In some pleasant rustic nook,
I shall mellow old with Nature
With a calm and peaceful look.

I shall have a garden round it
With a path among the trees;
Three grapevines shall I plant there
Morning glories and sweet peas.

I shall breathe the air of blossoms
And imbibe of nature's flask;
Cultivating thus God's friendship,
Death should be a trivial task.

For one's sun should set serenely
In a sky of rosy red
And in peace one's soul should sink
To its calm celestial bed.

James Gordon O'Neill

40- Canada Secure

Thanks to the parting ocean,
By the Almighty planned,
E'en fore he made the land
Or had set this earth in motion.

Thanks to our peaceful neighbours,
Situated near and far;
That without fear to mar
We may reap of peaceful labours.

Thanks to our generous God,
For minerals under ground,
For fish and forests found,
Fertile soil in every clod.

To all aggressive nations,
Deluded all the while,
We fling a firm denial:
"Strength's not armed populations."

1936

41- Winter's Resurrection

O winter, thou seemest akin to us mortals
By clinging so fast to each fleeting day
For fear thou be swallowed in Death's dark portals
And be wafted remotely to regions away.

Thy life-span extendeth to April's brink.
Why dost thou exceed thy rightful allotment?
Is it fear of the unknown makes thee shrink
Or hast thou ambitions short of fulfillment?

For, like man, if he quit this mundane sphere,
Shall quickly transcend his mortal form,
Thou, at thy death (assuage thy fear)
Shall be joyfully resurrected to Springtime warm.

42- Calamatas Civitatis

I sat content without a care
When looking out the window there.
Ere long, I saw two ladies fair;
This rhyme I wove from that same pair.

Perambulator one did wheel,
A sense of joy her heart didst feel;
On leash, the other, led at heel,
A small, black dog, her heart's appeal.

Affection, truly, both possessed;
With love, forsooth, both were obsessed.
Actions of each need not be guessed;
Baby and dog were both caressed.

Baby's birthright is lady's breast;
'Gainst "puppy" love I do protest.
For things are now a sorry pass,
When dogs can charm a pretty lass.

1936

43- The Drought

In the window, nose against the pane,
Poor feverish girl, she looks and waits;
While, inwardly, her heart debates,
If ever he will come again.

In the summer through the lengthy drought,
Sad burning Earth peers up to heaven,
Hoping 'gainst hope, the clouds will open;
Embrace her. Since so long in doubt.

44- Grubs and Grub

Abel, lone and sickly
Gunless, sought his forest food,
—Fev'rish, famine-wasted form—
In a Venezuelan wood.

Leaf-stalks, roots and berries,
Congealed gum and small birds' eggs;
Food found, wild but scanty,
Helped sustain his languid legs.

Great grubs white and wiggly
Roasted o'er some rotten wood,
Huge grubs, hot and juicy,
In his hunger tasted good.

Back home hale and hardy
Cooking o'er a modern range,
Beefsteak, hot and juicy,
To his mem'ry tasteth strange.

1937

45- Expression

He sought to vent his saddest mood;
Rid melancholy, long repressed.
His pen, he straightway hath addressed,
And writ in great solicitude.

Expression gave his soul relief,
And utterance hath his mind appeased;
Poetic instinct him hath siezed
And borne away his morbid grief.

Then think not sorrow always hard,
Nor all is bad as doth appear,
When thou, perchance, art hovering near
The sovereign regions of the bard.

1937

46- Blessed are the Humble

That man who serves unselfishly
Will master all eventually;
Great thoughts, great deeds, great works of art,
Are seldom wrought by selfish heart;
Less chance there is to reach his aim
For him who works for self and fame
Than camels go through needles' eyes
Or wolves for lambs pass in disguise.

Forsake thyself and thou shalt find,
When life is fully duty-lined,
Thou, universal thoughts, canst pen
And common maxims bring to men;
Canst sculpture cut from coldest stone
With human warmth and beauty shown;
Till bye and bye comes sweet success
That all posterity will bless.

46-a. A Winter's Dying Thrust

A snowstorm at the end of March
Is stubborn Winter's dying thrust;
Unwittingly, his drifting gust
Erects the Spring's triumphal arch.

A shower, which at April's dawn
Rejuvenates the ancient earth,
Proclaims the welcome Springtime's birth
And manifests that Winter's gone.

47- A Lament

Can it be I was reared as a lad on the land,

On a good fertile farm in the Township of Dawn,

Where the best things of Nature and all that is grand,

Could be got for the getting and had at first hand;

That, forsaking the plough, yet a youth, I am gone

To seek fame midst the maze of Metropolis Grand,

And compete in the market of men, for command

Of a house on a lot with one tree in the lawn?

After less than ten years in this urban turmoil,

I would welcome the day I could plough the old field

With its well-known rock; its familiar old oak.

These inanimate things and the rich tangy soil

Are more friendly by far and more pleasure will yield

Than sidewalks and sewers and cool city folk.

1937

48- Autumn

Neath the mellowing autumn sun
The tasselled corn its ears has borne;
Its purpose won, and duties done,
Stands daily praying to be shorn.

Behold, e'er now, o'er southern mere
How harvest fields give up their yields;
The stubbles sere show now quite clear
That death its sceptre gently wields.

Then comes good grateful farmer paul;
Death, personified, stoops beside
These corn stalks tall, proud martyrs all;
Ere sun has set they all have died.

May God the garnerer of all—
Our souls matured, our faith assured—
Be quick to call in early Fall,
Spare us cruel age, so hard endured.

1936

50- Shall These Things Be

Is this a proper thing to see
In our fair and loved countrie;
Lives reduced to paupery
So many doomed to misery?

Is this a Christian nation then,
Or a race of godless men;
Principles in slavery
While our babes go hungry?

Is it a fitting thing to do
On a Sunday morning, too;
Crowds carousing on the sand
Covered by a single strand?

With youth and maiden drinking beer
Is it not a time to fear?
Decency and morals sink
Whene'er a nation turns to drink.

Should one man live in a hovel slum,
Where the cold his bones benumb,
While his neighbour there, so callous,
Dwells within his marble palace?

Are these things still to be;

Can we not the evil see?

Governments have now the power

If they would but serve the hour.

Rise up an save our land from wreck,

Fix a firm and certain check;

Save our progeny from doom,

Let better days begin to loom.

1936

51- Finnish Courage

The Finnish clime is cold,
And Finnish snow is deep,
And in the frozen Finnish hold
The Russians huddle in a heap.

The Finnish men are brave
And Finnish hearts are stout.
They call Red Stalin "Knave"
And put his hordes to rout.

And Finland bears no grudge
And Finns no malice bear,
Thus, all the world may judge
For whom to offer prayer.

52- Roses

Though rosebuds hold potential pleasure
The full rose brings the final measure;
This compact bit of beauty rare
Will be 'ere soon, a full rose fair".

A human, seldom Reason's child,
Bore up his head and sagely smiled:
"The full rose yields not half the joy
Of little rosebuds round and coy,

For soon the blown rose waxes old
And downward droops toward the mould—
Its bloom, become but Beauty's wraith,
Speaks not of Beauty, but of Faith."

1937

53- Driving Westward

Ahead October's sky does glow—a glorious sight,

A fitting setting for the great sun's bier;

Magnificent the sight presented here,

As west we sped before the coming night.

What harmony of tint and shade and tone!

What greys and flares of hue do there enshroud

Yon little solitary tuft of cloud,

As great king Sol descends from off his throne!

Lifting their heads above yon great high hill,

The stalwart pines, with long straight whorled bough,

In silhouette contrast with trees deciduous;

And lest you think man's contribution nil,

Mark how yon, distant, towering smoke-stack now

Points out the first bright evening star to us.

1935

54- Oh, Tardy One

A man there is whom many hate,
That man, who always makes one wait;
Who still retains his steady gait,
Full well he knows he'll make you late.

I cannot help but relate,
How once, it fell to be his fate
To have with Kate a heavy date;
'Twas she he wished to make his mate.

The date he knew had called for eight,
But nine would do, and Kate could wait.
So, when he came to Kate's estate,
She had run out with other bait.

So men take care and ne'er be late,
If you wish to keep your mate
And be esteemed at highest rate,
'Mongst men and women small and great.

1936

55- Two Opinions

Shall we escape both wind and cold,

Be free of all the snow of old;

How can this present winter pass

And not conceal last summer's grass?

For now the season's halfway through,

The old folks' courage grows anew;

They recollect that, years before,

One Winter skulked right by their door.

The young express resentful feelings,

And slander winter for such dealings;

When will they use those skates and sleds

St. Nicholas left beside their beds?

1937

56- A Tree with a Dying Limb

A tree with a dying limb
Is a spectacle quite grim;
For the thought of it haunts
And the sight of it taunts.

It speaks of a coming end
When the tree and the dust will blend;
For the tree, that now shades
Both the dust and the blades,

Will lie lower that either;
Be distinguished from neither;
Ere a few seasons pass,
'Twill be one with the grass.

Death does not smite at one blow
But stealthily creeps on its foe;
Right form birth it begins
Till it finally wins.

If some man shall deliver
This old elm need not wither;
What a shame it would be
Not to save this fine tree!

Come, then, save its life

With trowel, saw or knife,

Lest it shade no more soon

Bird or beast, at high noon.

1936

57- The Struggle

Whilst Thor held Earth in his fierce and mad embrace,

His cloudy vestments veiled his flaming face.

Save times she squirmed, mid meek embarrassment,

He bared his brow to view his harassment;

And whilst his flashing gaze scissored heaven's vault,

He loosed his thund'rous voice in mad assault

And raging rumblings from his nostrils boomed.

T'was then his poor trembling victim, cowed and doomed,

Wobbled wildly in her starry course

And struggled valiantly to withstand his mighty force.

Then by sudden intervention comes a mighty hush

And poor quivering Earth revived with a fev'rish flush.

1995

58- Return Of Spring

I have lived to greet another spring
(An octogenarian's dream come true).
After the cruel winter I've been through,
What joy this season will surely bring.

The raucous crow that caws all day;
The honking goose that forms a V;
The cardinal whistling from a far-off tree;
They all say that Spring has come our way.

And if you must seek for further proof:
The first robin removes all doubt
That laggard Spring is here about;
And snow has melted off every roof.

And now that Spring is truly here,
All things in Nature will soon revive,
And every being rejoice to be alive;
Both young and old hold life most dear.

1996

59- Martyrs by Choice

Weary women, worn and wan,

Why so weary and woe-begone?

Why these melancholy features,

When, once, you were such happy creatures?

We are sacrificing teachers;

Do not blame us for our features.

We martyr for the boys and girls

At once, both little saints and churls.

We will forbear our proper share

Of earthly joys and pleasures fair;

We will renounce a family hearth,

But grant us first our proper worth;

We will not murmur nor complain

But leave us to our queenly reign.

Our thrill and happiness doth come

From only partly pleasing some

Of all the fond parental persons

From highland Scotch MacPhersons

To doting Dutch Van Dusens

And Irish Pat's and Susan's.

1937

60- Spring

Early Spring is like a shy child
Peaking from behind its mother's skirts;
With some days cold and others mild,
Earth is only warmed in little spurts.

As the child becomes more bold
And ventures forth from mother's care,
Steadily the days become less cold,
And warmth is felt most everywhere.

And by the twenty-fourth of May,
It sheds all parental charge.
With courtship of the sun by day,
Spring smiles upon the world at large.

1996

61- The Pending Storm

Earth's dome grows dark as the clouds scud past
And lightning scissors across the vault;
Wild Thor dins out a thunderous blast
And all nature joins the grand assault.

The cows in formation stand, tails to the storm;
The colts kick their heels to show how they feel;
The children in delirious delight perform
All the antics they can devise and deal.

The birds scurry for shelter in tree or eave;
The dog whimpers and slinkily crawls under the table;
The old folk pull down the blinds and believe
They have taken all the precautions they are able.

Then comes a quiet hush and a mighty stillness
In which all nature lies in suspended animation;
The whole earth has developed a mysterious illness
To which only rain drops can bring resuscitation.

1996

62- Belshazzar

Belshazzar, the king made a feast
That Babylon's court might applaud
As they drank form the cups of the priest
That belonged in the temple of God.

In that hour came forth a man's hand
That wrote as alive on the wall
And it traced on the plaster as sand
The idolatrous king's early fall.

Belshazzar beheld on the wall,
Beheld on the wall of his room,
Was forced to behold in that scrawl
The sign of his imminent doom.

A decree went forth from the king,
Went forth form the palace that night;
For no solace could anyone bring
As his knees smote together in fright.

Whilst the king of Babylonia trembled
Caldean astrologers came;
And nomadic magicians assembled
To exhibit their quack and their fame.

They studied in vain for a star
For none could interpret the sign
That appeared to the lords and Belshazzar
When the thousand caroused with their wine.

Belteshazzar, a captive of Judah
Came forth on request of the queen;
This Daniel, inspired by Jehovah,
Made known what the writing did mean.

"Belshazzar, O king, thou art weighed,
Art weighed in the balance of life,
For the worship of gods thou hast made
With chisel and mallet and knife.

Consider the rise and the fall
Of Nebuchadnezzar, thy sire,
How God set him up over all
And deposed him again in his ire.

Thou, O king, hast not humbled thy heart,
And God, in whose hand is thy breath,
At whose voice kingdoms rise and depart,
Hath decreed thy immediate death."

Wickedness doth destruction breed;

His wine and his idols were vain;

His kingdom was seized by the Mede;

In that night King Belshazzar was slain.

63- The First Pasture

One smiling morn in sunny May,
The stock stand munching tough dry hay;
Outside the fence their eyes can feast
On fresh green grass just meant for beast.

The farmer knows their hearts' desires
And frees them from enclosing wires,
For since it is the twelfth of May
He yearly pastures on this day.

The winter calves when first set loose
Seem not to miss their captive noose,
Stiff-legged they stand and smell the earth,
—First sense of freedom since their birth.

The captious colts bend back their ears
And chase and tease the cowering steers.
|The older horses snort and race
With tail in air, and wind in face,

And as they circle through the trees,
They stop by times to sniff and wheeze;
The old milch cows kick up their heels
And each one like a yearling feels.

An ant-hill which is in that spot,
One moment is and then is not;
For quickly as the bull arrives
Upon that hill his fury drives.

He strikes and paws terrific blows
Then snorts and sniffs it with his nose;
Down to his knees the monster must
To rub his brisket in the dust.

While many of his kind look on
He wallows till his wind is gone
Exhibiting his strength and might,
Oblivious of the poor ant's plight.

To taste new pleasure once again,
He leaves the first with much disdain,
And, as if his will were satisfied,
He shuffles off with portly pride.

He courts his host of humble kine
At cropping pasture short and fine,
Till filled, they wander through the brush,
To browse amidst the forest's hush.

1937

64- The First Robin

Go tell your neighbours;
Go tell your kin;
You have seen a robin,
First harbinger of spring.

Sing welcome to that bird
Whose cheerful notes are heard
From every lawn and orchard tree,
To every hill and distant valley.

Go tell your neighbours;
Go tell your friends;
Robin redbreast heralds spring:
The time when cruel winter ends.

Speak gleefully of that bird
Whose cheerful notes have stirred
Sweet memories of the past
And anticipation of spring at last.

1996

65- The Old Man With The Scythe

At eighty-seven years of age,

What do the coming months presage?

One knows 'tis great to be alive;

How can my cunning somehow contrive

To shun the "OLD MAN WITH THE SCYTHE"?

'Tis best to keep a happy mien;

Let not frustrations e'er be seen;

For when your birthday next comes round

And you're still alive and safe and sound:

Thumb your nose at the old man with the scythe.

1996

66- Nubbins

Sorrow is but a governor
Set upon the wheels of time
By an omnipotent creator
To make our joys sublime.

***

Canadian youth will cling to truth
Tenacious as a bull-dog's tooth;
If right is done and honour won,
'Twill be by a Canadian son.

***

Nobleness shines like a gem
Set in a lovely diadem;
Humility, a silent grace,
Softens the furrow of any face,

***

When I think of the castle of Shane
'Tis a feeling of pride the I feel;
Sure, I'm back in old Ireland again
Mongst the ancient clan of O'Neill.

***

On the periphery of consciousness
Lie myriad songs of loveliness;
If circumstance could give them birth,
New lays would wake the weary earth.

***

Intent, each day, new things to know
Men seldom prize familiar things
And fail to feel the joy life brings
As through the years they blindly go.

***

If we're faced with weal and woe
As through life we daily go,
Let our woes be bravely met
Then, strangely, all is "weal" yet.

***

Behaviourists and atheists prepare
For death may come to you unaware;
Deny immorality then, my friends;

Say not that with death the righteous life ends,

For, when our soul has fled to its maker,

Our body only, goes to the undertaker.

***

Crying, we are hurled

Into this cold, dismal world;

Sobbing still, many pass out,

Never free form sorrow and doubt.

Few men understand

How to live to make life grand;

Drifting on with no ideal,

The sensual is all they feel.

***

And now that death is drawing on

And light of day is almost gone,

What hast thou done of any worth

To merit life upon this earth?

And that death is drawing nigh

And days of life are nearly by

What will you do of any worth

To merit life upon this earth?

***

On the broad periphery of consciousness
Lie myriad unsung poems of loveliness;
But were some circumstances to call them forth
New songs would ring of classic worth.

***

I have laboured hard in the work shop of life
I have fashioned a body and fashioned a soul;
I am toiling today to perfect my products;
Form the latter for Heaven; the first off the dole.

***

Sorrow is but a governor
Set upon the wheels of time
By an omnipotent creator
To make our joys sublime.

It is the catalyzing agent
That helps us all to cope,
Till our being effervesces
With pleasure, joy and hope.

1937

67- The Last Peach

Could this be my very last peach?
Or shall I another season reach?
I cannot know, I cannot guess;
I can but hope that God will bless.

At ninety years, 'tis very clear
I haven't long to stay here;
But let this last fruit taste good
And may I enjoy it as I should.

Let this not be my very last peach!
Oh Lord, of you, I do beseech;
For I still have visions of things to do:
Please do not make my days too few.

27/09/99

68- Bank Phobia

Stephan Leacock is dead and gone
But still his humor carries on;
For whenever I enter a bank
I'm sure to feel of inferior rank.

While I have money in their trust
I still get the feeling that I'm bust;
And I must consult my deposit box
To make sure I'm not on the rocks.

I tremble to have my book updated
Lest the balance be less then anticipated;
And if, as often happens, it's in the red
The more my bank is a place to dread.

Some day when the lottery has made me rich,
(Or the stock market; I care not which)
I'll enter that bank, a calm cookie,
Deposit my fortune and prove I'm no rookie.

26/07/01

69- The Joy Of Paying Taxes

Receipt of a Canada Revenue letter

Makes me feel I am a debtor.

Immediately I become perplexed

And wonder what will happen next:

For I can't stand another whack

Like the one in their last clawback.

It was a temporary war-time tax

But no government dares give it the axe:

Possessed of such a lucrative cow,

It will be forever permanent now.

Making out a tax form is a chore

Few people can do any more;

Without an accountant they're lost

And engage one - hang the cost.

On every purchase, sale or fee

We must calculate the G.S.T.:

On every man, woman, girl or boy

It spreads its all-inclusive joy.

Since these taxes are here to stay,

We have no recourse but to pay;

Let us do it with a cheerful face

And make our payments with good grace.

11/8/01

Write your own Poetry

Write your own Poetry

Write your own Poetry

•

Write your own Poetry

Write your own Poetry

Write your own Poetry

Write your own Poetry

Write your own Poetry

Write your own Poetry

Write your own Poetry

Write your own Poetry

.

Write your own Poetry

Write your own Poetry

Write your own Poetry

About the author

James Gordon O'Neill brings a broad human perspective to his poetry. His first glimpse of light in 1909 showed a much simpler world. Since then, James is an eyewitness to the complexity of life growing at an exponential rate. As a farm boy growing up in Lambton County in Southern Ontario, James remembers seeing his first airplane fly over his home, which the neighbors proclaimed surely to be a German spy plane. James recalls the first automobile on their dirt road and then his father buying their first car, a MacLaughlin Buick. James experienced life during WWI, the roaring twenties, the stock market crash. He survived the lifestyle of the great depression, WWII and all the world developments and technological marvels since. He witnessed firsthand the great leaders of the twentieth century and the notorious ones, all the time living his own life and values.

The career of James O'Neill covers a wide spectrum. As a young farmhand he determined that viewing the back-end of a plough horse was not his lot in life. Guidance from his father Harry O'Neill was simple…"Jim, I can't afford to send you to university so you'll have to go to normal school (teachers' college). Later he added BA and B.Ped degrees. His teaching career took him from his home area of Dawn Township, to Windsor Ontario and then Toronto. He was promoted to vice-principal and then principal. After 40 years in education, James 'retired' and went into real estate sales, selling development land around the burgeoning metropolis of Toronto.

James met his wife-to-be when he attended teachers' college in London Ontario and boarded with William and Nellie Corless whose daughter Marjorie also became a teacher. James and Marjorie enjoyed a long and model marriage and were a major strength to each other. They have 3 children, 4 grandchildren and 1 great grandchild.

James' career then saw him as a caregiver in Marjorie's last years in which she lost her sight. Since her passing in 1995 James has resumed his writing career. He earlier wrote his memoirs, "OF OTHER DAYS AROUND ME". Poetry writing first occupied James in the 1930's when he and Marjorie lost a child at birth.

James O'Neill's poetry reflects life in the complex twentieth century with a view toward the simpler sights, sounds and joys in the midst of harsher realities.

Printed in the United States
4071

9 780759 688162